Here Comes BioDyslexia! The Commander of the Dyslexia Defenders!

A Guide to Empowering Dyslexic Heroes, Unleashing Their Potential, and Soaring to Extraordinary Heights

Sri Juliana Safri

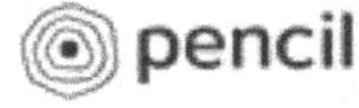

ISBN 978-93-5883-043-9
© Sri Juliana Safri 2023

Published in India 2023 by Pencil

A brand of
One Point Six Technologies Pvt. Ltd.
Unit no. 26, Ground Floor, Building A1,
Wadala Truck Terminal Road,
Near Post Office, Antop Hill, Mumbai - 400037
E connect@thepencilapp.com
W www.thepencilapp.com

All rights reserved worldwide

No part of this publication may be reproduced, stored in or introduced into a retrieval system, or transmitted, in any form, or by any means (electronic, mechanical, photocopying, recording, or otherwise), without the prior written permission of the Publisher. Any person who commits an unauthorized act in relation to this publication can be liable to criminal prosecution and civil claims for damages.

DISCLAIMER: *The opinions expressed in this book are those of the authors and do not purport to reflect the views of the Publisher.*

Author biography

Dear Reader,
Welcome to the captivating realm of " Here Comes BioDyslexia! The Commander of the Dyslexia Defenders!"

As an enthusiastic explorer of the dyslexic mind, a devoted mother to nine extraordinary children, three of whom possess the remarkable gift of dyslexia, and a passionate teacher guiding dyslexic students toward their full potential, I am thrilled to embark on this awe-inspiring journey with you.
This book holds a special place in my heart, as it was indeed born from the depths of my teaching experience and personal journey as a mother. The countless hours spent in the classroom, witnessing the triumphs and challenges of dyslexic students, have left an indelible mark on my soul. Moreover, supporting my own children through their unique learning journeys has fueled my determination to create a world where every dyslexic individual is celebrated and empowered.

It was through the amalgamation of my teaching experiences and personal encounters as a mother that BioDyslexia came into being. This initiative was born out of a burning desire to bridge the gap between dyslexic individuals and the world around them. I wanted to create a comprehensive resource that would not only provide practical guidance but also inspire hope, foster understanding, and ignite a sense of empowerment.

Within the vibrant pages of " Here Comes BioDyslexia! The Commander of the Dyslexia Defenders!," I intend to weave together my personal experiences as a mother and educator with a tapestry of knowledge and insights gained from walking alongside dyslexic individuals on their educational odyssey. It is my fervent belief that every child, regardless of their learning differences, deserves a world where their uniqueness is cherished, their strengths are amplified, and their voices are heard.

Through the sharing of practical strategies, evidence-based interventions, heartwarming stories, and profound insights, I aspire to empower both educators and parents alike. Together, we can build a solid foundation of knowledge, empathy, and support to uplift dyslexic individuals and help them thrive in their academic pursuits and personal lives.

" Here Comes BioDyslexia! The Commander of the Dyslexia Defenders!" is not just a book; it is a movement. It is a rallying cry to society, urging us to recognize and celebrate the immense potential that lies within each dyslexic individual. It is a call to action for educators, parents, and communities to create inclusive environments that foster growth, ignite passion, and unleash the hidden talents of dyslexic learners.

I invite you, dear reader, to embark on this exhilarating and fun expedition alongside me. Let us forge a future where dyslexic students are not only understood but embraced for their extraordinary talents and contributions. Within the pages of " Here Comes BioDyslexia! The Commander of the Dyslexia Defenders!," you will find a beacon of guidance, a reservoir of encouragement, and a wellspring of empowerment to unleash the full potential of your child or students and create a classroom that radiates with acceptance and possibility.

Together, let us champion the cause, shatter barriers, and pave the way for a world where dyslexic individuals can soar with confidence, realizing their dreams and leaving an indelible mark on our ever-evolving society.
Are you ready to embark on this remarkable expedition, dear reader? Let us embark on this transformative journey of "BioDyslexia" where the extraordinary becomes the norm, and the impossible becomes achievable.

With boundless excitement and unwavering dedication,

Julie Safri

CONTENTS

Epigraph

To my incredible family and unwavering support team (you know who you are!)

This book is dedicated to all of you. Your love, support, and unwavering belief have been my inspiration. Thank you for standing by me and for showing me the power of resilience. This book is a testament to our shared journey and a beacon of hope for others facing similar challenges. May Allah bless us and guide us always!
With heartfelt appreciation,

Your forever cheerleader, your guiding light, and your biggest fan!

Introduction

Step into the extraordinary world of "BioDyslexia," where the pages come alive with hope, knowledge, and the power to transform lives. Dyslexia may be a formidable foe, but armed with the right tools and a sprinkle of innovation, we can rewrite the narrative and unlock the true potential of dyslexic individuals.

In this literary adventure, we embark on a quest to unravel the mysteries of dyslexia, peering into its intricate causes and elusive symptoms. "BioDyslexia" is your compass, guiding you through the labyrinth of understanding, emphasizing the importance of early detection and intervention. We shed light on the profound impact that timely support can have on the learning journey of dyslexic individuals, as they navigate the maze of academia.

But fear not, for our quest does not end there! We journey deeper, unveiling the magic of "BioDyslexia" itself. This innovative fusion of structured learning and biofeedback holds the key to unlocking hidden potential. Through carefully crafted learning programs and the power of biofeedback protocols, we tap into the immense cognitive abilities of dyslexic individuals. Our book unveils a treasure trove of detailed protocols and scripts, enabling you to implement biofeedback seamlessly into a comprehensive dyslexia treatment plan.

Yet, "BioDyslexia" is more than just an intervention program—it is a beacon of support and understanding. We venture into the realms of home and educational environments, where we mold nurturing spaces for dyslexic individuals to flourish. Assistive technologies emerge as steadfast companions, offering aid in daily tasks. But we don't stop there; we delve into the emotional and social challenges that dyslexic individuals may encounter, equipping readers with practical strategies to navigate through stormy waters. With each turn of the page, we reveal the secrets to developing effective study skills, sharpening reading abilities, and mastering the art of written expression.

As our dyslexic heroes march forward on their educational and professional paths, "BioDyslexia" stands by their side, a beacon of guidance in the face of adversity. We weave tales of triumph and showcase inspiring narratives of dyslexic individuals who have soared to great heights in various fields. The stories of their success serve as reminders that dyslexia is not a barrier but a unique trait that can be harnessed to fuel extraordinary achievements.

Join us on this transformative journey as we illuminate the power of structured learning, biofeedback, and a supportive community. With "BioDyslexia" as your steadfast companion, you will gain the knowledge, tools, and inspiration needed to empower dyslexic individuals, enabling them to conquer challenges, embrace their strengths, and rewrite their destinies. Together, let us unveil the hidden superpowers within each dyslexic soul and witness them soar to their full potential.

Dyslexia Decoded The Mysterious Adventures of Twisted Letters and Wandering Minds

Dyslexia, oh dyslexia, the trickster of language and reading! It's like having a secret code that only dyslexics can decipher, and boy, does it keep us on our toes. But fear not, for in the land of learning, there is hope and support aplenty!

This condition, with its mischievous ways, can make reading, writing, and understanding a bit of a rollercoaster ride. It sticks around for a lifetime, like that one friend who never seems to leave the party. School and everyday life become a challenge, as if dyslexia thought it was playing an epic game of hide-and-seek with our brains.

Yet, amidst this linguistic labyrinth, if we catch dyslexia in its sneaky act and lend a helping hand, wonders can happen. Early detection is key, my friends! Just like a superhero sensing danger, spotting dyslexia in its early stages lets us unleash the powers of assistance and guidance. And boy, can people with dyslexia soar to unimaginable heights when equipped with the right tools!

Here Comes BioDyslexia! The Commander of the Dyslexia Defenders!

The origins of dyslexia remain as mysterious as a masked vigilante. It's a mix of genes and the world around us, like a cosmic soup of factors. It often runs in families, passing down its linguistic legacy from one generation to another. Certain genes take center stage, influencing the development and functioning of those language-loving parts of our marvelous brains.

Now, each dyslexic hero is unique, with their own set of superpowers and quirks. But fret not, there are some common signs to keep an eye out for! Beware of the troubles of sounding out words, the spelling conundrums, and the slow and bumpy reading journeys. Blending sounds can be an elusive feat, and remembering words might feel like trying to catch smoke with a net made of spaghetti. Ah, the struggle of extracting information from the depths of our minds and wrestling with putting thoughts onto paper!

But hold tight, dear readers, for dyslexia's powers extend beyond the realms of language. It can cast its spell on math, attention, and memory as well. Like a mischievous sorcerer, dyslexia loves to sprinkle its challenges far and wide, making school a battlefield and taking a toll on self-esteem.

But fear not, for united we stand! Early detection is our guiding light, leading us to the path of tailored support and assistance. When dyslexia reveals itself during those tender years of preschool or early school, BioDyslexia activates specialized programs to sharpen those reading skills. And believe me, dear comrades, this makes all the difference!

Parents, teachers, and a league of supportive allies band together to ensure our dyslexic champions receive the help they need. Special skills are taught, granting them the power to conquer sounds and words with finesse. We unleash the mighty arsenal of multisensory learning, engaging our senses like a symphony of knowledge—touch, sight, and hearing joining forces. Extra time for tests and assignments becomes a fair play rule, leveling the playing field for our valiant warriors. And let us not forget the wonders of technology! BioDyslexia aims to address not only the challenges associated with reading and writing but also delve deeper into the inner realms of your heart and mind. Our approach goes beyond mere linguistic skills, seeking to understand and support the holistic well-being of individuals

In our realm of learning, we craft a sanctuary—a haven where dyslexic souls can seek aid and feel the warmth of support. We celebrate their strengths and nurture their unique talents, for within their extraordinary minds lie gifts waiting to be unwrapped.

Armed with knowledge, armed with tools, BioDyslexia transforms the battlefield into a stage for success. Dyslexia may be a formidable foe, but together we shall prevail! With early detection and unwavering support, our dyslexic warriors will rise, reaching their goals and claiming victory.

So be at ease, dear readers, for dyslexia, may be a riddle, but we hold the answers. Let us embrace the challenge, armed with empathy and understanding, and empower our dyslexic comrades to embark on their heroic journey of triumph!

15

Superhero Senses Early Detection and Intervention for Dyslexia - Saving the Day Before the Battle Begins!

In the ever-unfolding chapters of our dyslexia odyssey, we now embark on a critical quest: the significance of early detection and intervention. Brace yourselves as we dive into the depths of this essential journey, where timely support can shape the destinies of dyslexic individuals.

Research has illuminated a profound truth: early detection holds the key to brighter futures. By identifying dyslexia in its infancy, during the preschool or early elementary years, we can swiftly initiate targeted interventions tailored to the unique needs of these individuals. The impact is nothing short of miraculous, as early intervention not only improves reading skills but also prevents secondary difficulties that may arise from untreated dyslexia.

At the heart of early detection lies the art of systematic screenings. Through the use of screening tools, we can identify children who may be at risk for dyslexia based on their early reading and language abilities. These assessments delve into the depths of phonological awareness, letter knowledge, and rapid naming skills. By regularly monitoring these foundational skills, educators can discern which children may benefit from further evaluation and targeted interventions.

Comprehensive assessments serve as the compass that guides us to a confirmed dyslexia diagnosis. These assessments cast a wide net, encompassing reading accuracy, fluency, comprehension, and the evaluation of phonological processing skills and cognitive abilities. A multidisciplinary approach, drawing upon the expertise of psychologists, speech-language pathologists, and educational specialists, ensures a holistic understanding of the individual's unique profile.

Early intervention programs, tailored specifically to the needs of dyslexic individuals, emerge as the champions of reading and language development. These programs encompass structured and explicit instruction in phonological awareness, phonics, vocabulary, and reading comprehension. By bestowing targeted interventions at an early stage, educators empower dyslexic individuals to construct a solid reading foundation while minimizing the negative impact that dyslexia may have on their academic trajectory.

Yet, early intervention transcends the realm of academia alone. It extends its benevolent reach to the realm of socio-emotional well-being. Dyslexic individuals may find themselves grappling with frustration, anxiety, and dwindling self-esteem due to their struggles with reading and writing. It is within the nurturing embrace of a supportive environment, crafted by educators and parents alike, that their confidence and resilience are fostered. Involving dyslexic individuals in self-advocacy and celebrating their strengths and talents further nurtures their overall well-being.

The benefits of early detection and intervention stretch far beyond the boundaries of the classroom. By addressing dyslexia in its infancy, individuals can develop effective compensatory strategies and adaptive skills that will accompany them throughout their lives. With appropriate interventions and accommodations, dyslexic individuals can achieve academic success, pursue their passions, and flourish in every facet of their diverse lives.

As we turn the page to the forthcoming chapters, we will explore a myriad of structured learning approaches by BioDyslexia, including multi-sensory techniques and assistive technologies. These invaluable tools shall find their rightful place within educational settings, seamlessly integrating with the fabric of support for dyslexic individuals. By weaving together the threads of early detection, targeted interventions, and a supportive environment, we shall empower dyslexic individuals to transcend their challenges and embrace their boundless potential.

Stay tuned, dear readers, for the adventure continues. The journey towards embracing dyslexia as a unique gift unfolds before us, beckoning us to unlock the extraordinary within.

Are you seeing signs? Here's a mini-screening that can help detect potential signs of dyslexia or raise red flags for further assessment. It's important to note that this screening should not be considered a definitive diagnosis, but rather a tool to identify potential areas of concern:

Please tick the appropriate box for each statement:
Letter and Sound Recognition:
Can recognize uppercase and lowercase letters of the alphabet:
☐ Yes ☐ No
Phonological Awareness:
Can identify and manipulate individual sounds in words:
☐ Yes ☐ No
Word Reading:
Can read age-appropriate words with ease:
☐ Yes ☐ No
Spelling:
Can spell common words accurately:
☐ Yes ☐ No
Reading Comprehension:
Can understand and answer questions about a short passage:
☐ Yes ☐ No
Reversals and Confusions:
Frequently reverses letters or numbers or confuses visually similar ones:
☐ Yes ☐ No
Writing Skills:
Can write legibly and accurately:
☐ Yes ☐ No

- Please note that this screening is intended as a preliminary tool and not a definitive diagnosis. If a child shows persistent challenges in multiple areas, it is recommended to seek a comprehensive assessment by a qualified professional to determine the presence of dyslexia or other learning differences.

Cracking the Dyslexia Code BioDyslexia Structured Learning Approaches That Turn Learning into a Grand Adventure!

Welcome to the enchanting realm of teaching dyslexic individuals, where structured learning techniques and multi-sensory marvels await. In this chapter, we shall unveil the secrets of BioDyslexia that will pave the way for dyslexic individuals to become exceptional readers, writers, and communicators.

One powerful approach is centered around phonics and decoding skills, emphasizing letter-sound correspondences, syllable types, and blending strategies. By engaging dyslexic individuals through a delightful blend of visual, auditory, and kinesthetic elements, we ensure a comprehensive learning experience that caters to their unique needs.

Another effective method involves BioDyslexia's structured curriculum that progresses from foundational skills to more advanced reading and spelling strategies. Through direct instruction, repetition, and reinforcement, dyslexic individuals can enhance their phonological awareness, decoding abilities, and encoding skills.

Comprehensive instructional modules cover various components like phonics, fluency, vocabulary, and comprehension. They use a structured sequence of lessons that build upon each other, reinforcing key concepts and skills. Creating a structured learning environment with consistent routines, clear instructions, and manageable task breakdowns lays the foundation for success.

Visual aids such as charts and graphic organizers can help organize information and enhance understanding. Regular practice and review are essential for reinforcing learning and promoting knowledge retention. Technology also plays a supportive role, with educational software, apps, and assistive technologies providing interactive experiences that reinforce reading and writing skills.

By implementing these structured learning approaches and utilizing supportive resources, educators can create an inclusive environment that caters to the unique needs of dyslexic individuals. These approaches provide explicit instruction, reinforcement, and practice opportunities, empowering dyslexic learners to become confident readers and successful learners.

So, fellow adventurers, let us embark on this journey of BioDyslexia and unlock the boundless potential that lies within dyslexic individuals. Together, we shall illuminate the path to literacy triumph and pave the way for a future where all dyslexic learners can thrive.

Unlocking the Senses BioDyslexia Multi-Sensory Magic for Dyslexia Intervention and Supercharged Learning

Prepare to unleash your super senses on an extraordinary adventure of learning! With the power of BioDyslexia's multi-sensory approaches, dyslexic learners become the mighty heroes of literacy, conquering challenges with their superhero abilities.

Behold the visual marvels that await! Visual aids become their trusty sidekicks, guiding them through charts, diagrams, and color-coded cues, unveiling hidden knowledge with every glance. Their eyes become laser beams of focus, absorbing information like superheroes scanning their surroundings.

But listen closely, for the auditory symphony begins! Dyslexic learners harness the power of sound, repeating and practicing sounds, syllables, and words with heroic determination. Like sonic superheroes, their ears become finely tuned receptors, detecting the nuances of language and transforming them into their arsenal of words.

With a touch of greatness, kinesthetic and tactile techniques come into play. They shape letters and words like sculptors of language, their fingers becoming nimble heroes that bring language to life. Every movement and every touch fuel their learning journey, leaving a tactile imprint of their superhero prowess.

In the digital realm, multi-sensory computer programs become their mighty allies. These technological wonders fuse visual spectacles, captivating sounds, and interactive adventures, transforming dyslexic learners into digital superheroes. Their screens become portals to knowledge, where they harness the power of literacy with a single touch.

Rise and Shine Building Dyslexic Superpowers - Self-Esteem and Resilience Edition!

Once upon a time in the magical realm of dyslexia, we gather around the round table of knowledge to unveil the secret powers that lie within dyslexic individuals. Join us on this whimsical adventure as we unravel the mysteries of self-esteem and resilience, and discover the fantastical abilities that make dyslexic superheroes shine brighter than a shooting star!

Dyslexia, often seen as a challenge, becomes a source of inspiration and empowerment when individuals discover the superpowers hidden within.

The first step in this heroic transformation is fostering a supportive and inclusive environment. Educators, parents, and peers join forces to create a sanctuary of understanding and acceptance. By shedding light on the incredible abilities that dyslexic individuals possess, we cultivate a culture of appreciation and celebration.

Recognizing and honoring the superpowers of dyslexic individuals is essential for building their self-esteem. Whether they possess extraordinary creativity, problem-solving skills, or exceptional interpersonal intelligence, their talents are acknowledged and celebrated. Through encouragement and positive reinforcement, their self-worth soars, propelling them to new heights of confidence and resilience.

Equipping dyslexic individuals with the tools they need is the next phase of their superhero training. Assistive technologies, personalized learning plans, and tailored classroom adjustments level the playing field, enabling them to excel academically. Armed with these resources, their confidence soars, and they feel empowered to conquer any academic challenge that comes their way.

Developing a growth mindset is a crucial component of their superhero journey. Emphasizing the power of effort, practice, and continuous growth, they view obstacles as stepping stones to success. With an unwavering belief in their potential and the resilience to persevere, they rise above setbacks and emerge stronger than ever.

Empowering dyslexic individuals to advocate for themselves is a pivotal step on their heroic path. Equipped with self-awareness and self-advocacy skills, they fearlessly articulate their needs and seek appropriate support and accommodations. By reclaiming control over their education and daily lives, they unlock a newfound sense of confidence and agency.

But they do not embark on this journey alone. A united dyslexic community stands as an unbreakable alliance. Peer support, mentorship programs, and support groups provide a network of understanding and validation. Together, they share experiences, strategies, and triumphs, forging an unbreakable bond that combats isolation and inspires collective growth.

In their quest for self-mastery, dyslexic individuals learn the art of mindfulness and stress management. Armed with techniques to navigate challenges, regulate their emotions, and prioritize self-care, they become resilient superheroes. Through resilience, they conquer adversity, maintain unwavering positivity, and relentlessly pursue their goals.

The transformation from self-doubt to self-belief requires the combined efforts of educators, parents, peers, and individuals themselves. By nurturing an inclusive environment, celebrating strengths, fostering a growth mindset, and providing tailored support, dyslexic individuals unleash their inner superheroes.

Together, we embark on the next chapters, exploring additional strategies to elevate their self-esteem, resilience, and overall well-being.
For within the hearts of dyslexic individuals lies a superhero waiting to emerge, a hero capable of rewriting their destiny, and an inspiration to others on their path to greatness.

Biofeedback The Secret Weapon Against Dyslexia's Evil Plot to Mess with Words

In this mind-boggling chapter, get ready to uncover the mind-bending technique of biofeedback and its mind-altering potential in the world of dyslexia! Brace yourselves for a journey into the realm of technological marvels that will have you saying, "I can't believe it's not magic!"

So, what's the buzz about biofeedback and why is it a game-changer for dyslexic individuals? Picture this: you become the master of your own body, equipped with the ability to regulate and optimize your internal processes. It's like having a superhero's control panel for your body, where you can fine-tune your cognitive powers and unleash your true potential!

Biofeedback involves using cutting-edge devices and sensors to monitor your heart rate, brainwaves, and even the sweat on your skin. It's like having a team of mini detectives inside you, gathering valuable clues about how your body responds to different situations. And the best part? You get real-time feedback presented to you in mind-blowing ways, like visual displays and sound effects that will make you feel like you're in a sci-fi movie!

Here Comes BioDyslexia! The Commander of the Dyslexia
Defenders!

By harnessing the power of biofeedback, individuals with dyslexia can tap into their body's secrets, gaining control over their attention, relaxation, and overall brain function. It's like having a mental gym membership, where you can pump up your brain muscles and achieve cognitive greatness!

But wait, there's more! Biofeedback is here to save the day when it comes to those pesky attention issues. Ever feel like your brain is playing tag with distractions? With biofeedback, you'll learn techniques to level up your focus and keep distractions at bay. Say goodbye to wandering thoughts and hello to a supercharged concentration that would make even the most focused heroes jealous!

Biofeedback is also a hero when it comes to battling stress and anxiety, which can sometimes feel like sneaky villains lurking in the shadows. But fear not, as biofeedback techniques will arm you with the skills to conquer stress and achieve Zen-like calmness. Your brain will thank you for the vacation from those stress-induced villains!

Now, get ready to enter the realm of neurofeedback, the biofeedback technique that focuses on training your brain's electrical activity. It's like controlling a video game with your mind! Using a fancy device called an electroencephalogram (EEG), your brainwaves will be measured and analyzed, providing feedback on your brain's performance. You'll embark on a mind-bending adventure where you'll teach your brain epic new tricks to enhance attention, memory, and other mind-blowing cognitive skills that will level up your reading and language abilities!

But remember, biofeedback isn't a standalone superpower. It works best when combined with BioDyslexia's evidence-based learning approaches we've explored earlier. It's like forming a superhero dream team that takes dyslexia by storm!

So, are you ready to unlock the potential of your mind? Biofeedback sessions are typically conducted by super-skilled professionals like psychologists or BioDyslexia's biofeedback therapists. They'll design a training program tailored to your specific goals, and you'll be the star of the show, determining the duration and frequency of your sessions.

In the upcoming mind-bending chapters, we'll dive deeper into mind-blowing biofeedback techniques and exercises that will make you the true superhero of your mind. Get ready to embrace the power of biofeedback, unleash your cognitive abilities, and soar to new heights of learning and achievement. It's time to become the dyslexic superhero you were always meant to be!

Biofeedback Unleashing Your Inner Hero - Upgrading Your Brain for Superhuman Abilities!

Get ready to discover even more fascinating information about biofeedback that can supercharge learning for people with dyslexia! It's like having a personal coach for your body, giving you real-time updates on how it's doing. By bringing biofeedback into the mix, we can give dyslexic individuals an extra boost on their learning journey.

Biofeedback Unveiled: Let's dive into the world of biofeedback. It's like having a secret spy that tells you what's happening inside your body. We'll unravel how it works, explore the different types of biofeedback, and see how it can be a game-changer for dyslexic learners. Get ready to uncover the hidden signals of your body!

Finding the Perfect Fit: Now it's time to figure out which biofeedback measurements are most helpful for dyslexia. We'll look at things like heart rate, skin sweatiness, breath speed, and even brainwave activity. These measurements give us clues about how our body and mind are doing, like having a personal health tracker for learning.

Turning Learning into Fun and Games: Brace yourself for some fun-filled learning adventures with biofeedback! Imagine reading a book while your heart rate cheers you on or doing relaxation exercises that make your skin share its chill vibes. These activities help you become more self-aware and boost your learning powers, especially if you have dyslexia. Learning just got a whole lot cooler!

Team Up for Success: Bringing biofeedback into BioDyslexia learning programs is a team effort. Teachers, parents, and dyslexic learners need to join forces. We'll show you how to train and support everyone involved, like a squad working together. From learning the tricks of biofeedback technology to making sure everyone feels confident and supported, it's a united mission.

Cracking the Code of Progress: Biofeedback isn't just about fancy gadgets; it's about decoding the messages your body sends. We'll uncover the secrets of data analysis, finding patterns, and linking physical reactions to learning outcomes. It's like being a detective investigating what works best for each individual. Prepare to unravel the mysteries of progress!

Respect Boundaries and Staying Safe: Whenever we step into the realm of technology and personal information, we must prioritize ethics and privacy. We'll talk about getting consent, keeping things confidential, and safeguarding biofeedback data. It's all about creating a safe and respectful environment, like having a bodyguard for your privacy.

Real-Life Tales of Triumph: Get ready for some inspiring stories about real people with dyslexia who have embraced biofeedback and reaped its rewards. These stories showcase the transformative power of biofeedback, like having superpowers for learning and well-being. Get ready to be inspired by these dyslexic superheroes!

By bringing biofeedback into BioDyslexia's learning journey, we unlocked new levels of learning for individuals with dyslexia. It's like having a turbo boost for learning, empowering them to take control of their bodies, focus better, and feel amazing along the way. Get ready to level up!

Biofeedback Protocol & Script Unleash Your Inner Jedi - Mastering the Force of Mind Control!

In this super awesome chapter, we're going to unveil a top-secret biofeedback protocol specially designed for our dyslexic pals who want to level up their attention and focus game. Prepare for some mind-boggling techniques that will make distractions tremble in fear and concentration soar to new heights!

Picture this: dyslexic individuals donning their biofeedback capes, ready to conquer the challenges of staying focused. We kick things off by giving them a "superpower assessment" to identify their attentional nemesis. We're talking attention span, distractibility, and task-switching skills—our heroes won't leave any stone unturned!

Now, time to bring in the fancy gadgets. We've got heart rate monitors and EEG-based systems at our disposal, like something straight out of a superhero movie. Each gadget serves a unique purpose, depending on the specific attention skills we're targeting. It's like assembling a team of gadgets, each with its superpower!

During the BioDyslexia therapy sessions, our dyslexic heroes will receive real-time feedback about their physiological responses. It's like having a personal coach whispering in their ears, saying, "Hey, your heart rate is racing! Focus, my friend!" It's a biofeedback bonanza that will make them more aware of their attentional rollercoaster and help them make the necessary adjustments.

But wait, there's more! We're not just here to throw gadgets at them. Our heroes will learn epic techniques to regulate their attention and keep distractions at bay. From mastering the art of deep breathing (imagine them taking deep breaths like a yoga guru!) to conjuring up mental images that captivate their focus, they'll become attention superheroes in no time.

And here's the best part: their attention skills won't just be confined to the therapy sessions. Oh no! We're unleashing these skills into their everyday lives. Whether they're studying, doing homework, or fighting evil math problems, they'll have the power to create a distraction-free learning environment. It's like having their fortress of solitude where distractions dare not enter!

But remember, even superheroes need sidekicks. That's why we have a team of trained professionals by their side, guiding them every step of the way. These professionals are like the Alfred to their Batman or the Happy Hogan to their Iron Man, ensuring they reach their full attention potential.

So gear up, dyslexic heroes! Get ready for a biofeedback adventure that will make your attention soar to new heights. With your focus sharpened like a laser beam, you'll conquer the reading world and achieve cognitive greatness. It's time to unleash your inner attention superhero and save the day!

Emotionally Empowered Hero Mastering Stress with BioDyslexia Biofeedback Heroic Protocol!

In a world where stress and anxiety run rampant, even our beloved dyslexic superheroes can face their share of challenges. But fear not! We present to you BioDyslexia biofeedback protocol & script designed to help these incredible individuals conquer stress and master emotional regulation.

Picture Dyslexic Dynamo, with a cape made of heart rate, monitors and a utility belt adorned with electrodermal activity sensors. Together, they embark on a mission to empower dyslexic individuals to manage their stress responses and cultivate emotional resilience.

The adventure begins with an assessment phase, where Dyslexic Dynamo evaluates stress levels and identifies those pesky triggers that make life extra challenging. Armed with self-report measures, observations, and insightful conversations, our hero uncovers the sources of stress and crafts a personalized training plan.

Equipped with biofeedback devices like heart rate monitors and electrodermal activity sensors, Dyslexic

Dynamo conducts therapy sessions that would make any supervillain shake in their boots. These nifty gadgets measure physiological indicators of stress and emotional arousal, providing real-time feedback to dyslexic individuals. Imagine the thrill as they witness their stress levels and emotional states right before their very eyes!

During the therapy sessions, our dyslexic heroes dive into relaxation exercises, embracing the power of deep breathing, progressive muscle relaxation, and guided imagery. As they practice these techniques, the biofeedback devices serve as trusty sidekicks, revealing heart rate, skin conductance, and respiratory patterns. This instant feedback allows our heroes to fine-tune their relaxation strategies and level up their stress-busting game.

Armed with newfound knowledge, Dyslexic Dynamo's protégés learn to recognize the early warning signs of stress and anxiety. As their heart rate speeds up or muscles tense, they tap into their inner superpowers and use biofeedback cues to initiate relaxation responses. Through practice and determination, they become masters of their physiological responses, achieving emotional balance and resilience. It's like watching a superhero origin story unfold right before our eyes!

But the adventure doesn't end there. To ensure success, it's crucial to incorporate stress management strategies into everyday life. Dyslexic Dynamo guides their proteges in time management skills, problem-solving strategies, and positive self-talk. They create a supportive environment where communication flows freely and outlets for relaxation, such as physical activity or artistic expression, are abundant. After all, even superheroes need a break and a chance to unwind!

With the collaborative efforts of trained professionals, educators, and parents, the BioDyslexia biofeedback therapy process becomes a dynamic team effort. These superheroes work together, guiding dyslexic individuals to harness the power of biofeedback techniques effectively and monitoring their progress. Educators and parents provide unwavering support, reinforcing stress management strategies within academic and home settings. It's a united front, ensuring that no dyslexic hero fights alone.

But remember dear readers, practice makes perfect! Dyslexic individuals are encouraged to apply stress reduction and emotional regulation techniques in real-life situations, both in and out of the classroom. With dedication and consistency, they can unlock their true potential, overcome stress-related barriers, and embark on a journey toward enhanced well-being.

So, embrace your inner Dyslexic Dynamo, and let the quest for stress reduction and emotional resilience begin!

Do you want to Unleash Your Inner Attention Hero? Take the Biofeedback Superhero Focus Challenge!

Answer each question based on your superhero experience. Choose the response that best reflects your abilities.

When facing a task, I find it easy to maintain focus and resist distractions.

a) I'm a laser-focused superhero!

b) I can stay focused most of the time.

c) I get distracted occasionally.

d) My attention is easily diverted.

My mind tends to wander during missions that require sustained concentration.

a) My mind is as sharp as my superhero senses!

b) I can stay focused for a while, but sometimes my mind wanders.

c) I struggle to maintain focus for long periods.

d) My mind constantly wanders off track.

It is effortless for me to stay focused on a task for an extended period.

a) I have the ultimate attention superpower!

b) I can stay focused for a good amount of time.

c) It's challenging for me to stay focused for long.

d) I quickly lose focus and switch between tasks.

I rarely get distracted during a mission or when solving problems.

a) Distractions have no power over me!

b) I can usually stay on task, but distractions occasionally get to me.

c) I struggle to resist distractions and stay focused.

d) Distractions constantly derail my concentration.

My superhero heart beats calmly and steadily during intense missions.

a) My heart is as steady as a superhero's pulse!

b) My heart rate remains stable most of the time.

c) My heart rate increases occasionally during intense tasks.

d) My heart races and affects my ability to concentrate.

Now, let's calculate your biofeedback superhero score. Assign the following points for each response:

a) I'm a laser-focused superhero! - 4 points
b) I can stay focused most of the time. - 3 points
c) I get distracted occasionally. - 2 points
d) My attention is easily diverted. - 1 point

Add up your points for all the responses, and refer to the interpretation below:

15 to 20 points: You possess exceptional superhero attention skills!

10 to 14 points: Your superhero focus is generally strong, with occasional room for improvement.

5 to 9 points: Your superhero attention abilities could benefit from biofeedback training.

1 to 4 points: You may struggle with maintaining superhero-level focus, and biofeedback techniques could greatly enhance your abilities.

- Remember, this mini-test is for illustrative purposes only and does not replace a formal evaluation or medical advice, and it doesn't replace a formal evaluation or professional advice. Enjoy discovering your superhero attention skills!

The Dyslexia Defenders Unleashing the Extraordinary Powers Within!

In the realm of superpowers, there exists a hidden gem known as "The Dyslexia Advantage"! Imagine a world where dyslexic individuals harness their incredible abilities to save the day in the most extraordinary ways. While their arch-nemesis may be reading and spelling, these superheroes rise above the challenges and showcase their unique talents.

Meet our first hero, Creativo! With an imagination that knows no bounds, Creativo can conjure magnificent art, design awe-inspiring architecture, and engineer mind-boggling structures. Their superpower lies in visual and spatial reasoning, allowing them to create jaw-dropping masterpieces that leave everyone in awe.

In the city of Novamore, there was a young artist named Clara. She had a big imagination and could create amazing art, stunning architecture, and mind-boggling structures. People called her Creativo, and she had a special power. She could visualize things in her mind and make them real.

One day, the city's beautiful fountain stopped working. The people were sad and wanted it to be fixed. Creativo heard about this and decided to help. She went to the fountain and closed her eyes. She imagined a magnificent sculpture that would tell a story of unity and harmony.

With her special power, Creativo started to change the fountain. She used her hands to make invisible shapes and lines in the air. Bit by bit, the fountain transformed into a breathtaking masterpiece. Water flowed down in beautiful patterns, and colors sparkled in the sunlight. The people were amazed and grateful. After that, Creativo became the city's hero of art. She used her imagination to make the city's buildings and streets look incredible. People from all over the world came to see her creations. The city became a place of art and creativity.

But Creativo didn't do it just for herself. She wanted to inspire others to be creative too. She taught workshops and helped other artists. She wanted everyone to know that they could make beautiful things with their imagination.

As time went on, Creativo's influence spread. Her ideas became a part of the city's identity. She became an old artist, but her legacy lived on. People remembered her as someone who used art to make the world a better place.

So, the story of Creativo, the city's first hero, was told for many years. It was a story of imagination, amazing art, and the belief that art can change the world.

Here's a short test designed to assess a child's creative abilities and imaginative thinking, inspired by the traits of Creativo:

Artistic Expression:

Provide the child with a blank canvas and a set of art supplies. Encourage them to create unique artwork that represents their favorite place in the world. Observe their use of colors, shapes, and imagination in conveying their chosen location.

Architectural Marvel:

Give the child a collection of building blocks or Legos and ask them to design and construct their dream structure. Encourage them to think beyond conventional buildings and let their imagination run wild. Observe their creativity, attention to detail, and ability to create something unique.

Inventive Storytelling:

Ask the child to come up with an original story using their imagination. Provide a few prompts or themes to choose from, such as "A magical adventure in a secret garden" or

"An unexpected encounter with a friendly alien." Assess their storytelling skills, originality, and ability to create a captivating narrative.

Transformative Art:

Present the child with a random object, such as a cardboard box or a plain wooden frame, and challenge them to transform it into something completely different using their creativity and craft supplies. Observe their ability to think outside the box and their resourcefulness in repurposing everyday objects.

Imaginary World:

Ask the child to draw or describe an imaginary world of their creation. Encourage them to include unique landscapes, fantastical creatures, and any other elements that showcase their limitless imagination. Assess their ability to visualize and articulate their imaginative ideas.

Collaborative Creation:

Pair the child with a friend or family member and provide them with a joint creative task, such as building a mini-city or designing a costume. Observe how well they collaborate, exchange ideas, and combine their talents to create something amazing.

- Observe the child's approach, originality, and ability to think outside the box to assess if they demonstrate the traits of Creativo. Keep in mind that this test is just a starting point and should be adapted based on the child's age and abilities. The aim is to gauge their creative thinking, imaginative skills, and their enthusiasm for expressing themselves through various artistic mediums.

Next up, we have Brainwave! Armed with exceptional problem-solving skills, Brainwave can crack the toughest puzzles and unravel the trickiest riddles. Their ability to think outside the box and approach tasks from unconventional angles make them the go-to hero for any perplexing situation. No enigma stands a chance against Brainwave!

In the bustling city of Enigmaville, there lived a remarkable individual named Alex. While others saw puzzles and riddles as mind-bending challenges, Alex saw them as thrilling adventures waiting to be conquered. Gifted with exceptional problem-solving skills, Alex became known as Brainwave, the city's go-to hero for any perplexing situation.

Brainwave possessed a remarkable ability to think outside the box. When faced with a puzzle, he would delve into the depths of his mind, exploring unconventional angles and innovative approaches. No enigma could withstand the power of Brainwave's intellect.

Word quickly spread throughout Enigmaville about Brainwave's uncanny knack for cracking the toughest puzzles. Whenever the city faced a mystery that seemed unsolvable, the citizens knew exactly who to call. Brainwave would arrive, his mind is sharp and ready for the challenge.

In one such instance, a mischievous criminal had hidden a precious artifact somewhere in the city. The people of Enigmaville were in despair, unable to decipher the intricate clues left behind. But Brainwave stepped forward, his eyes gleaming with determination.

He examined each clue meticulously, analyzing every word, symbol, and hidden meaning. While others struggled to connect the dots, Brainwave's mind worked like a well-oiled machine, piecing together fragments of information to form a coherent picture.

Where others saw chaos, Brainwave saw patterns. He ventured into uncharted territories of thought, exploring ideas that others deemed impossible. With each step, he unraveled the threads of the puzzle, inching closer to the truth.

Finally, after hours of relentless thinking and exploring, Brainwave unlocked the final clue. He deciphered the intricate web of hints and revealed the location of the hidden artifact. The people of Enigmaville erupted in joy and gratitude, marveling at Brainwave's exceptional problem-solving abilities.

As time went on, Brainwave's reputation grew, and his services were sought far beyond Enigmaville. He would travel to neighboring cities, cracking codes, solving mysteries, and bringing closure to those in need.

But Brainwave never let his exceptional skills go to his head. He remained humble and approachable, always ready to lend a helping hand. He would often hold puzzle-solving workshops, inspiring others to tap into their problem-solving potential.

The city of Enigmaville flourished under Brainwave's guidance. His knack for unraveling the trickiest riddles brought a sense of wonder and excitement to the community. Children and adults alike admired Brainwave's intellect and aspired to cultivate their critical thinking skills.

And so, Brainwave continued his journey as the hero of Enigmaville, leaving no enigma unsolved. With exceptional problem-solving abilities and his willingness to think outside the box, he brought clarity to the most perplexing situations, ensuring that the city thrived on the power of intellect and curiosity.

Here's a short test designed to assess a child's problem-solving abilities and unconventional thinking skills, inspired by the traits of Brainwave:

Present the child with a few riddles that require creative thinking to solve. Include riddles that have multiple possible answers or require thinking beyond the obvious.

Challenge 1: Riddle Expedition

Embark on a journey of riddles that require out-of-the-box thinking. Uncover the hidden answers and explore multiple possibilities. Can you solve these brain-teasers?

"Whispering Winds: What am I?"
"The Mysterious House: How to Determine Occupancy?"

Whispering Winds: *The answer is "echo." An echo is something that can "speak" without a mouth, "hear" without ears, and is created when sound waves bounce off surfaces.*

The Mysterious House: *To determine if someone is home in a house with all the lights turned off, you can knock on the door and listen for any sounds or footsteps inside. If you hear a response or movement, it indicates that someone is likely home.*

These riddles are designed to challenge their thinking and encourage them to explore different possibilities. Well done if they were able to solve them!

Challenge 2: Unconventional Quest

Gear up for an unconventional problem-solving adventure! Get your hands on building blocks and create a gravity-defying structure to balance an egg. Or dive into the world of shapes and transform them into a brand-new object. The choice is yours!

Challenge 3: Pattern Detective

Become a master pattern detective! Decode hidden sequences of numbers and images. Identify the underlying pattern and predict the missing element. Sharpen their pattern recognition skills with these intriguing challenges:

"Number Expedition: 2, 4, 6, 8, __"
"Vowel Voyage: A, E, I, __"

Challenge 4: Thinking Beyond Boundaries

Break free from the ordinary! Confront puzzles that require innovative thinking. Imagine retrieving a rooftop ball without ladders or climbing equipment. Discover unconventional ways to cross a river without boats or bridges. Challenge their imagination and find alternative solutions!

Challenge 5: Mind-bending Conundrums

Prepare for mind-bending conundrums that will put your logical reasoning to the test. Divide a cake into eight equal pieces with just three straight cuts. Explore how a single matchstick and a table tennis ball can create an upright marvel. Are you up for these perplexing challenges?

Embrace the adventure, and observe how your approach, creativity, and ability to think beyond the obvious unfold. This test is designed to unleash your inner Brainwave, assessing your problem-solving skills, unconventional thinking, and eagerness to explore new possibilities. Let the journey begin!

Say hello to Spectra! Armed with the power of visual thinking, Spectra can instantly perceive patterns, connections, and complex concepts. They have an innate ability to see the big picture, making them an invaluable asset in decoding cryptic messages and unraveling mysterious plots. Spectra's mind is a kaleidoscope of knowledge!

In a whimsical land of imagination and wonder, there lived a superhero named Spectra. Spectra possessed a special gift that made her truly extraordinary — she could see and understand things in a unique and enchanting way.
Spectra's power was all about seeing patterns, connections, and hidden wonders in the world around her. She could gaze upon a dazzling rainbow or a field

of blooming flowers and instantly grasp the magic within. It was as if the world whispered secrets of beauty to her!

One sunny day, Spectra discovered that her powers extended beyond just seeing colors. She could also envision the extraordinary in ordinary objects and transform them into fantastical creations. A simple cardboard box became a pirate ship sailing the vast seas, and a collection of pebbles turned into a shimmering treasure trove. Her imagination knew no bounds!

Spectra loved to express her creativity through art that made people smile and dream. With her unique ability, she could create stunning paintings, intricate sculptures, and marvelous inventions. Her artwork became a portal into her vibrant imagination, inviting others to join in the enchantment.

But Spectra's powers didn't end there. She had a special talent for solving puzzles and riddles. Whenever her friends faced a perplexing challenge, they would seek Spectra's guidance. Spectra could uncover hidden patterns and uncover clues that led to the solutions, becoming the hero of every puzzle!

Children from far and wide adored spending time with Spectra. They would eagerly bring their drawings, puzzles, and dreams to share with their superhero friend. Spectra would listen attentively, understand their hopes and aspirations, and use her magical mind to help bring those dreams to life.

Spectra's presence lit up even the gloomiest of days. She could transform rainy afternoons into whimsical adventures by conjuring magical realms through art and storytelling. Friends would gather around, captivated by the vivid images and captivating tales that only Spectra could create.

But Spectra knew that her powers went beyond creating beautiful art. She understood that colors and shapes carried their language, and through her imagination, she could express emotions and bring joy to others.

With her incredible powers of visual thinking, Spectra encouraged her friends to see the extraordinary in the ordinary. She inspired others to explore their creative talents, trust their unique visions, and find their touch of magic. Spectra showed everyone that art and imagination could transform the world in the most wondrous ways.

And so, Spectra, the superhero with the extraordinary gift of visual thinking, continued to weave her spell of wonder and inspire others to embrace their creativity. She reminded everyone that through art, imagination, and a sprinkle of Spectra's enchantment, endless possibilities awaited!

Here's a short test designed to assess a child's visual thinking and pattern recognition abilities, inspired by the traits of Spectra:

Spot the Difference:

Provide the child with two similar images and ask them to identify the differences between them. Include subtle variations that require careful observation and visual acuity. Assess their ability to notice details and perceive patterns.

Shape Connections:

Show the child a series of shapes or objects and ask them to identify the underlying connection or relationship between them. For example, present a triangle, a square, and a circle, and ask them to determine the common attribute. Assess their ability to recognize patterns and categorize visual elements.

Picture Sequencing:

Provide the child with a set of pictures depicting a story or sequence of events. Shuffle the pictures and ask them to rearrange them in the correct order. Assess their ability to comprehend visual narratives and organize information sequentially.

Visual Puzzles:

Present the child with visual puzzles, such as mazes or tangram puzzles, where they need to use their visual thinking to find a solution. Assess their ability to analyze spatial relationships, think ahead, and mentally manipulate objects or images.

Visual Memory Challenge:

Show the child a picture or a series of objects for a short period, then remove the visual stimuli and ask them to recall and describe what they saw. Assess their visual memory skills and their ability to retain and recall visual information accurately.

Abstract Pattern Completion:

Display an incomplete abstract pattern or design and ask the child to fill in the missing parts. Encourage them to use their imagination and logical reasoning to complete the pattern. Assess their ability to extrapolate and visualize missing elements.

Visual Analogies:

Present the child with visual analogies, such as a picture of a cat alongside an empty fishbowl, and ask them to identify the relationship between the two images. Assess their ability to make connections, conclude, and infer meaning from visual cues.

Observe the child's approach, accuracy, and speed in completing the tasks to assess if they demonstrate the traits of Spectra. Keep in mind that this test is just a starting point and should be adapted based on the child's age and abilities. The aim is to gauge their visual thinking, pattern recognition, and their ability to perceive connections and complexities in visual information.

Introducing Intuitus, the superhero with unrivaled intuition! With a mere glance, Intuitus can grasp the essence of any situation, making split-second decisions that save lives and thwart evil plans. Their intuition is sharper than a superhero's sixth sense, guiding them through even the most chaotic of circumstances.

Once upon a time, in a world filled with wonder and excitement, there was a superhero named Intuitus. With his incredible gift of intuition, he could understand things in a way that no one else could.

Intuitus had a special ability to quickly know what was happening around him, even without anyone telling him. He could sense when something was wrong or when someone needed help. His intuition was like a super radar that guided them through all sorts of tricky situations.

With his amazing intuition, Intuitus could make split-second decisions that saved the day. He could predict what might happen next and always made the right choices. His superpower helped them stop bad guys and protect innocent people.

But it wasn't just about fighting crime. Intuitus could also understand how people were feeling. He could tell when someone was sad, happy, or scared, even if they didn't say a word. This made him a fantastic friend who could offer comfort and support when needed.

Intuitus loved using his powers to help others. He would often lend a hand to those who were lost or confused, guiding them with their intuitive wisdom. His ability to see the best in people and understand their true intentions made them trusted and beloved heroes in their city.

Whenever there was a problem or a puzzle to solve, everyone would turn to Intuitus for help. He could see patterns and connections that others couldn't, which made him unbeatable at solving mysteries and riddles.

It was like he had a special supercomputer in his mind!

But even with all his amazing powers, Intuitus remained humble and kind. He knew that intuition was a gift that could be nurtured and improved. He practiced his skills every day, learning to trust his instincts and listen to his inner voice.

Kids everywhere looked up to Intuitus and dreamed of having such incredible intuition. They admired how Intuitus used his powers for good and helped others without hesitation. They knew that even though they might not have superpowers like Intuitus, they could still trust their intuition and make a difference in their special way.

And so, Intuitus, the superhero with the amazing gift of intuition, continued to use his powers to bring happiness and peace to the city. He showed everyone that with a little trust in themselves and a keen sense of intuition, anyone could become a hero in their own right.

Here's a short test designed to assess a child's intuition and decision-making skills, inspired by the traits of Intuitus:

The Animal Whisperer:

Present the child with a series of pictures or descriptions of animals and ask them to identify the emotions or messages they perceive from each animal. For example, "What do you think this cat is feeling?" or "What do you think this dog is trying to communicate?"

Mystery Box:

Place several different objects inside a box without showing them to the child. Ask the child to close their eyes and use their intuition to guess what each object might be based solely on touch. Encourage them to describe the feelings and shapes they sense.

Who Said It?

Read a set of quotes or short statements to the child, and ask them to intuitively match each quote with the person they believe said it. The quotes can be from famous individuals, fictional characters, or even family members.

Trust Your Gut:

Present the child with a series of scenarios where they have to make a decision. Encourage them to listen to their intuition and select the option that feels right to them. For example, "You're playing a game, and your friend suggests a different strategy. What do you feel like doing?"

Symbolic Connections:

Show the child a set of symbols or abstract images and ask them to intuitively associate each symbol with a specific meaning or concept. For instance, "What does this symbol remind you of? What does it represent to you?"

Observe the child's responses, their ability to trust their instincts, and their level of confidence in their intuitive decisions. Keep in mind that this test is just a starting point and should be adapted based on the child's age and abilities. The aim is to gauge their intuition, decision-making skills, and their ability to perceive deeper meanings and connections beyond the surface.

Last but not least, meet Dynamo! Fueled by an indomitable spirit, Dynamo possesses unwavering resilience and determination. They've overcome countless obstacles and setbacks, rising stronger every time. Dynamo's sheer willpower and ability to bounce back make them an inspiration to all, proving that even superheroes face challenges and triumph over them.

Once upon a time, in a world where superheroes roamed, there was a brave and determined hero named Dynamo. Dynamo had a heart filled with courage and an unbreakable spirit. He was a true inspiration to all, proving that superheroes faced challenges too, and could triumph over them.

Dynamo's journey began when he discovered his extraordinary powers. With a single touch, he could harness the energy from within and unleash it in magnificent ways. It was like having a lightning bolt inside him, ready to spark into action whenever needed.

But Dynamo's greatest strength wasn't just his superpowers – it was his unwavering resilience. No matter what obstacle or setback came his way, Dynamo never gave up. He faced each challenge with a determined spirit and a belief in himself.

One day, Dynamo encountered a villain who seemed unbeatable. The villain used tricks and traps to try and bring Dynamo down, but he never lost hope. With each defeat, Dynamo grew stronger, learning from his mistakes and finding new strategies to overcome the challenges.

As Dynamo faced his doubts and fears, he discovered that setbacks were just stepping stones to success. He embraced every failure as an opportunity to learn and grow. Dynamo's determination was like a flame that couldn't be extinguished, burning brighter with each setback he faced.

People in the city admired Dynamo's indomitable spirit and drew strength from his example. They saw that even superheroes faced tough times, but it was how they responded that truly mattered. Dynamo showed them that with determination and a positive mindset, anything was possible.

Dynamo's journey was not always easy, but he never let that discourage him. He knew that the road to success was filled with challenges, and it was his resilience that made him a true hero. His unwavering spirit inspired others to believe in themselves and their abilities.

Children looked up to Dynamo, seeing him as a role model. They saw that no matter how many times Dynamo fell, he always got back up, even stronger than before. He taught them the importance of perseverance and never giving up on their dreams.

And so, Dynamo continued to protect the city with his remarkable powers and unyielding spirit. He showed everyone, young and old, that with determination and resilience, they could overcome any obstacle. Dynamo proved that true heroes were not defined by their superpowers alone but by the strength of their character and their ability to rise above challenges.

Here's a short test designed to assess a child's resilience and determination, inspired by the traits of Dynamo:

The Tower Challenge:

Provide the child with a set of building blocks and ask them to build the tallest tower they can in a limited amount of time. After a few minutes, introduce a distraction or obstacle, such as a gentle gust of wind or a small disturbance, to see how the child responds. Observe if they remain focused, adapt their strategy, and persist in building the tower despite the challenge.

The Puzzle Marathon:

Give the child a challenging puzzle or a series of puzzles to solve. Encourage them to keep going even when they encounter difficult parts or get stuck. Observe their level of persistence, problem-solving strategies, and their ability to stay motivated throughout the puzzle-solving process.

The Obstacle Course:

Set up a mini obstacle course or a series of physical challenges for the child to complete. Include tasks that require balance, coordination, and problem-solving. Observe how the child approaches each challenge, their level of determination, and their willingness to try again if they don't succeed on the first attempt.

The Storytelling Journey:

Give the child a blank notebook or a few sheets of paper and ask them to write or draw a story about a superhero who faces many challenges but never gives up. Encourage them to showcase the superhero's determination and resilience in overcoming obstacles. Observe their creativity, storytelling skills, and their ability to convey the importance of perseverance.

The Positive Affirmation:

Engage in a conversation with the child about their dreams and goals. Encourage them to share what they would do if they faced obstacles along the way. Ask them how they would stay motivated and remind themselves of their strength and determination. Observe their self-belief, positive mindset, and ability to develop strategies to overcome challenges.

Observe the child's responses, their level of determination, their ability to bounce back from setbacks, and their overall perseverance throughout the tasks. Keep in mind that this test is just a starting point and should be adapted based on the child's age and abilities. The aim is to gauge their resilience, determination, and their ability to overcome obstacles with a positive and determined mindset.

Together, these dyslexic superheroes champion the cause of inclusivity and diversity. They remind us that our differences are what make us extraordinary. They stand tall as beacons of strength, using their powers to illuminate a world that embraces and celebrates everyone's unique gifts. By joining forces with the incredible power of "BioDyslexia," you can unlock the existence of these extraordinary superheroes. Within the realm of BioDyslexia, you will discover the true potential of dyslexic individuals and witness the emergence of these remarkable heroes. Join this alliance and witness the remarkable journey of dyslexic superheroes saving the day with their Dyslexia Advantage!

Welcome to the Superhero Traits Assessment!

This exciting test is designed to help you uncover which superhero trait best matches your unique qualities. By answering a series of questions and assigning scores to your responses, you'll discover if you possess the powers of Creativo, Brainwave, Spectra, Intuitus, or Dynamo. Get ready to embark on this thrilling journey of self-discovery! This test is suitable for everyone, so let's dive in and uncover your inner superhero!

Note: Assign the following scores to each answer:

Strongly Agree: +3
Agree: +2
Neutral: +1
Disagree: -1
Strongly Disagree: -2

1. I enjoy expressing my creativity through art, such as drawing, painting, or crafting. (Creativo)

2. I find solving puzzles and brain teasers challenging and enjoyable. (Brainwave)

3. I notice patterns, shapes, and colors in my surroundings and find them fascinating. (Spectra)

4. I often trust my gut feelings and intuition when making decisions. (Intuitus)

5. I never give up easily and persist in achieving my goals, even when faced with challenges. (Dynamo)

6. I love coming up with imaginative solutions to problems. (Creativo)

7. I enjoy analyzing information and finding logical solutions to problems. (Brainwave)

8. I can easily spot patterns and connections between different things. (Spectra)

9. I often rely on my instincts and feelings when making decisions. (Intuitus)

10. I am determined and resilient, and I bounce back quickly from setbacks. (Dynamo)

11. I enjoy engaging in artistic activities, such as writing stories or performing in plays. (Creativo)

12. I enjoy solving math problems and logical puzzles. (Brainwave)

13. I have a keen eye for detail and notice even the smallest changes in my environment. (Spectra)

14. I trust my intuition and believe it helps me make better decisions. (Intuitus)

15. I am known for my perseverance and never give up attitude. (Dynamo)

Calculate the total score for each superhero trait by adding up the scores for each question related to that trait. The superhero trait with the highest score will indicate the one the child aligns with the most. It's important to remember that this test serves as a guide, and individuals may possess traits from multiple superheroes. Encourage the child to embrace their unique strengths and talents while fostering their growth in the identified trait.

Confused about how to get the score? Let us give you an example!

Let's say we have a child named Alex who answers the questions as follows:

1. I enjoy expressing my creativity through art, such as drawing, painting, or crafting. (Creativo) - Agree (+2)

2. I find solving puzzles and brain teasers challenging and enjoyable. (Brainwave) - Strongly Agree (+3)

3. I notice patterns, shapes, and colors in my surroundings and find them fascinating. (Spectra) - Strongly Agree (+3)

4. I often trust my gut feelings and intuition when making decisions. (Intuitus) - Neutral (+1)

5. I never give up easily and persist in achieving my goals, even when faced with challenges. (Dynamo) - Agree (+2)

6. I love coming up with imaginative solutions to problems. (Creativo) - Strongly Agree (+3)

7. I enjoy analyzing information and finding logical solutions to problems. (Brainwave) - Agree (+2)

8. I can easily spot patterns and connections between different things. (Spectra) - Strongly Agree (+3)

9. I often rely on my instincts and feelings when making decisions. (Intuitus) - Agree (+2)

10. I am determined and resilient, and I bounce back quickly from setbacks. (Dynamo) - Strongly Agree (+3)

11. I enjoy engaging in artistic activities, such as writing stories or performing in plays. (Creativo) - Agree (+2)

12. I enjoy solving math problems and logical puzzles. (Brainwave) - Strongly Agree (+3)

13. I have a keen eye for detail and notice even the smallest changes in my environment. (Spectra) - Neutral (+1)

14. I trust my intuition and believe it helps me make better decisions. (Intuitus) - Agree (+2)

15. I am known for my perseverance and never give up attitude. (Dynamo) - Strongly Agree (+3)

To calculate the total score for each superhero trait, we add up the scores for the corresponding questions:

Creativo: 2 + 3 + 3 + 2 = 10
Brainwave: 3 + 2 + 3 + 3 = 11
Spectra: 3 + 3 + 1 = 7
Intuitus: 1 + 2 + 2 = 5
Dynamo: 2 + 3 + 3 + 3 = 11

In this example, both Brainwave and Dynamo have the highest scores of 11. It indicates that Alex aligns with the traits of Brainwave and Dynamo the most. However, remember that individuals can possess traits from multiple superheroes. Encourage Alex to embrace his unique strengths and talents in both problem-solving and resilience.

Unlocking Superpowers Building Dyslexic Heroes with Self-Advocacy Skills

In this chapter, we embark on a journey of self-discovery and empowerment for dyslexic individuals. We'll explore how they can become their superheroes by developing self-advocacy skills.

Throughout the previous chapters, we've learned about dyslexia, its unique challenges, effective intervention strategies, and the power of biofeedback. We've met incredible dyslexic heroes like Creativo, Brainwave, Spectra, Intuitus, and Dynamo, each with their special abilities.

Now, it's time for dyslexic individuals to step into their power and become heroes of their own stories. We'll guide them in understanding their strengths and weaknesses, building confidence, and embracing their unique abilities. By recognizing their potential, they can overcome obstacles and make their voices heard.

Effective communication is key to self-advocacy. Dyslexic individuals will learn how to express their thoughts, needs, and concerns clearly and assertively. They'll practice public speaking, engage in discussions, and enhance their communication skills to ensure that others understand and support them.

Understanding their rights and accommodations is another important aspect. By knowing the laws and policies that protect their educational rights, dyslexic individuals can advocate for the support they need. We'll provide them with the knowledge and tools to level the playing field and create an inclusive learning environment.

Building a support network is crucial on this journey. Dyslexic individuals will connect with peers, mentors, educators, and support groups who understand their experiences. Together, they'll share resources, experiences, and support one another, creating a strong community of advocates.

Goal-setting and planning will guide dyslexic individuals toward success. By defining their aspirations and outlining the steps needed to achieve them, they'll stay focused and motivated. They'll learn to navigate their educational journey with determination and purpose.

Taking initiative is a superpower in itself. Dyslexic individuals will learn to actively seek help and support. They'll initiate conversations with educators, discuss their challenges, and request appropriate accommodations. Through collaboration and exploration, they'll discover strategies and technologies that enhance their learning experience.

Self-confidence and resilience will be their shield against doubt and setbacks. Dyslexic individuals will celebrate their achievements, recognize their strengths, and develop a positive self-image. They'll face challenges with unwavering determination, knowing that they have the power to overcome any obstacle.

Lastly, continual self-reflection and growth are vital. Dyslexic individuals will assess their progress, seek feedback, and adapt their self-advocacy strategies. By constantly learning and evolving, they'll become even stronger advocates for their needs.

By embracing self-advocacy, dyslexic individuals become the authors of their educational journey. They transform their challenges into opportunities for growth and empowerment. Together with the Dyslexia Defenders and the wisdom gained from previous chapters, they'll create a future where every dyslexic individual can thrive and succeed.

Dyslexia Warriors Unite Nurturing Social and Emotional Skills with a Dash of Dyslexic Charm

In the world of dyslexic superheroes, nurturing social and emotional skills is as important as saving the day! Dyslexia may make reading and writing a bit challenging, but it also affects social interactions and emotions. That's why it's crucial to focus on developing these super skills, so dyslexic individuals can have awesome relationships, manage their feelings, and conquer social situations like true superheroes.

One powerful skill to nurture is empathy. Dyslexic superheroes can educate others about their unique abilities and challenges, helping everyone understand and create a supportive environment. When their friends and teachers empathize and communicate effectively, dyslexic individuals feel like the heroes they truly are!

Another super skill is self-awareness. Dyslexic heroes should learn to recognize and understand their emotions, strengths, and areas for growth. By reflecting on themselves and accepting who they are, they can develop a super-powered self-image and face emotional challenges head-on.

Communication is a mighty power too. Some dyslexic heroes struggle with expressing themselves, but with practice and support, they can become expert communicators! Engaging in discussions, presentations, or writing in a safe space helps them gain confidence and improve their communication abilities.

Building resilience is like having an impenetrable shield against emotional challenges. Dyslexic heroes need healthy coping strategies, like deep breathing or enjoying their favorite hobbies, to overcome stress. By expressing their emotions constructively and bouncing back from tough situations, they become unstoppable!

Social skills training is like a secret weapon for dyslexic heroes. They can learn how to understand social cues, read non-verbal communication, and put themselves in others' shoes. Role-playing and feedback help them master social interactions, make friends, and resolve conflicts like true champions.

And let's not forget about sidekicks and mentors! Dyslexic heroes can connect with older peers who have already conquered similar challenges. These experienced mentors provide valuable guidance and encouragement. Plus, joining support groups with other dyslexic heroes lets them share experiences, seek advice, and feel like part of a super-powered community.

But wait, there's more! Parents and caregivers are like the superhero headquarters. They play a vital role in nurturing social and emotional skills at home, promoting positive communication, and creating a loving environment. Teamwork with educators and professionals ensures a well-rounded approach to supporting dyslexic heroes' social and emotional development.

In school, including activities that promote empathy, self-awareness, communication, and teamwork is a fantastic strategy. Dyslexic heroes can show off their skills, build relationships, and create a supportive classroom environment where everyone can shine!

By nurturing these social and emotional skills, dyslexic heroes become unstoppable forces, not just in school but also in their personal and social lives. With their empathy, self-awareness, communication, resilience, and social competence, they conquer social challenges, build amazing relationships, and maintain their overall well-being. They truly save the day, both academically and emotionally!

The Battle Against Dyslexia's Arch-Nemesis Stigma and Misconceptions

The Dyslexia Defenders, led by their fearless leader BioDyslexia, take on their toughest enemy yet—Stigma and his army of Misconceptions. They're determined to fight against the wrong ideas people have about dyslexia. With their superpowers of knowledge and understanding, our heroes work together to change minds and make the world a better place for dyslexic people. Through exciting stories and helpful tips, this chapter shows kids how they can stand up against stigma and be superheroes for dyslexia acceptance!

Join the Dyslexia Defenders on their newest mission! They're facing a sneaky enemy called Stigma, who wants to make people think dyslexia is something bad. But our heroes know better! In this chapter, we'll discover how they use their special powers to fight Stigma and teach everyone the truth about dyslexia.

Meet Stigma and the Misconceptions: Stigma is a tricky villain who spreads false ideas about dyslexia. Our Defenders reveal his secrets and show us the tricks he uses to make people believe the wrong things. We'll learn that dyslexia has nothing to do with being lazy or not smart. It's a superpower of its own, with special ways of thinking and learning!

Using Superpowers: Knowledge, Understanding, and Helping Others: Our Defenders show us the power of knowledge, understanding, and helping others. They teach us all about dyslexia, how it affects the brain, and the awesome strengths dyslexic people have. By sharing stories and being kind, we can bridge the gap between dyslexic and non-dyslexic friends. We'll also discover how to stand up for dyslexia acceptance and be superheroes for a change!

Superhero Allies: Friends and Inclusive Communities: The Defenders know that working together is the key to defeating Stigma. They'll teach us how to build inclusive communities where everyone feels valued. We'll learn about the importance of having supportive friends, family, and teachers. Together, we can create a world where dyslexic people can shine!

Unleashing the Power of Learning: Education is a powerful weapon against Stigma. The Defenders will show us how teachers can help dyslexic students succeed by using special techniques and understanding their needs. We'll also learn about the cool tools and technologies that can make learning easier for dyslexic superheroes!

The Triumph of Acceptance: In the end, our Defenders inspire a big change in how people see dyslexia. They help everyone understand that dyslexia is not something to be ashamed of, but something to celebrate. With their superpowers and the support of their friends, they create a world where dyslexic superheroes can be themselves and reach for the stars!

Now it's your turn to be a Dyslexia Defender! Remember, dyslexia is a superpower, and everyone deserves to be accepted and understood. Spread the word, share your knowledge, and be a friend to dyslexic superheroes everywhere. Together, we can defeat Stigma and make the world a better place for everyone!

Forever Heroes Leaving a Lasting Legacy

Welcome to the final chapter of our incredible adventure! Join BioDyslexia and the mighty Dyslexia Defenders as we reflect on our journey and the impact we have made in the world. Our adventure has come to an end, but our journey is just beginning. We have learned so much about ourselves and about dyslexia along the way. We have seen that we are capable of great things, even if we have dyslexia. We have also seen that we are stronger together than we are apart. As we move forward, we know that we will face challenges. But we also know that we can overcome anything if we believe in ourselves and each other. We are dyslexic superheroes, and we are here to make a difference.

Look back at the challenges faced throughout our journey. The Dyslexia Defenders Creativo, Brainwave, Spectra, Intuitus, and Dynamo share stories of strength and resilience, reminding us that dyslexic individuals are true heroes.

Every person has a hero within them. BioDyslexia and the Dyslexia Defenders encourage you to embrace your unique strengths and abilities. Discover your passions, talents, and superpowers. When you believe in yourself and recognize your worth, you become a hero capable of achieving greatness.

Heroes leave a lasting impact on the world. Our heroes discuss how dyslexic individuals can leave their mark and create a legacy that inspires future generations. From sharing their stories and advocating for dyslexia acceptance to mentoring and supporting others, dyslexic individuals can make a profound difference. Explore ways to contribute to the dyslexia community and empower others on their journeys.

The Power of Unity: BioDyslexia and the Dyslexia Defenders emphasize the importance of unity. Together, we can create a world where dyslexic individuals are celebrated and supported. Learn how to build a network of allies, collaborate with others, and foster a sense of community. By working together, we can amplify our voices and create a society that embraces and values dyslexia.

A Call to Action! It's time to take action and make a difference. Our heroes challenge you to advocate for dyslexia acceptance in your communities, schools, and beyond. Whether it's raising awareness, supporting dyslexic individuals, or promoting inclusive education, your efforts matter. Each step you take brings us closer to a world where dyslexic individuals are recognized and celebrated for their unique talents.

In this heartfelt conclusion, BioDyslexia and the Dyslexia Defenders offers a message of hope. You are not alone on your journey. With support, you can achieve greatness and inspire others. Embrace the power of hope, for it is the fuel that drives us to create a brighter future.

Conclusion: As our adventure comes to a close, remember that you are a hero capable of leaving a lasting legacy. Embrace your strengths, celebrate your journey, and empower others along the way. Together, we can change the world and create a future where dyslexic individuals are forever recognized as the heroes they truly are.

Thank you for joining us on this extraordinary journey, and may your own hero's journey continue to inspire and uplift others.

Notes

Copyright© 2023 Sri Juliana Safri

ALL RIGHTS RESERVED. This book contains material protected under Copyright Laws and Treaties. Any unauthorized reprint or use of this material is prohibited. No part of this book may be reproduced or transmitted in any form or by any means, electronic or mechanical, including photocopying, recording, or by any information storage and retrieval system without express written permission from the author/publisher

Any references to historical events, real people, or real places are used fictitiously. Names, characters, and places are products of the author's imagination.

First printing edition 2023

www.ingramcontent.com/pod-product-compliance
Lightning Source LLC
LaVergne TN
LVHW020952200726

843508LV00004B/1405